LOVED BEYOND MEASURE
A 3-MINUTE DAILY DEVOTIONAL FOR TEEN GIRLS TO DISCOVER THEIR GOD-GIVEN IDENTITY & WORTH

EVELYN HOPE

Copyright © 2025 by Hope Books Ltd

All rights reserved.

No part of this book may be reproduced in any form or by any electronic or mechanical means, including information storage and retrieval systems, without written permission from the author, except for the use of brief quotations in a book review.

Scripture quotations marked (MSG) are taken from THE MESSAGE, copyright © 1993, 2002, 2018 by Eugene H. Peterson. Used by permission of NavPress. All rights reserved. Represented by Tyndale House Publishers, Inc.

Scripture quotations marked (NLT) are taken from the Holy Bible, New Living Translation, copyright © 1996, 2004, 2015 by Tyndale House Foundation. Used by permission of Tyndale House Publishers, Inc., Carol Stream, Illinois 60188. All rights reserved.

Scripture quotations marked (TPT) are from The Passion Translation®. Copyright © 2017, 2018 by Passion & Fire Ministries, Inc. Used by permission. All rights reserved. ThePassionTranslation.com

A Note from the Author: These messages are inspired by Scripture and written to reflect God's heart as revealed in the Bible. While these devotionals are not literal words from God, they are crafted to express the truths, promises, and love found in the Bible, communicating the depth of God's love for young women.

You might notice Scripture references in italics - these are like treasures you can look up and dive deeper into if you want to.

As this book uses British English, you may notice some familiar words spelled differently.

CONTENTS

Introduction	v
1. You Are Loved	1
2. You Are Safe	3
3. You Belong	5
4. You Are Beautiful	7
5. You Are Created for Joy	9
6. You Are Strong	11
7. You Are Mindful	13
8. You Are Gifted	15
9. You Are A Truth-Bearer	17
10. You Are Creative	19
11. You Are Kind	21
12. You Are Brave	23
13. You Are Held	25
14. You Are Accepted	27
15. You Are Unstoppable	29
16. You Are Patient and Persistent	31
17. You Are Generous	33
18. You Are Known	35
19. You Are Precious	37
20. You Are Forgiven	39
21. You Are Chosen	41
22. You Are Anchored	43
23. You Are Peace-Filled	45
24. You Are Not Alone	47
25. You Are Pure	49
26. You Are Special	51
27. You Are Noble	53
28. You Are Wise	55
29. You Are Free	57
30. You Are Cherished	59
31. You Are Enough	61
Your Story Continues	63

An Invitation	65
One More Thing	67

INTRODUCTION

Welcome to this journey of discovering who you truly are!

Each day, you'll read a love letter straight from God's heart to yours. These messages are grounded in the Bible, which shows us exactly who He is and who we are in Him.

You can read these 3-minute devotions in the morning or in the evening. There's no right time to spend time with God - just find a time that works for you.

Some days, these truths might feel easy to believe. Other days, they might seem harder to accept. That's okay. God's truth about who you are remains constant, whether you're having a good day or a bad day.

He knows you, loves you, and delights in you just as you are.

So, as you begin, know that you are already deeply loved and completely accepted by God.

With love,

Evelyn

1
YOU ARE LOVED

My precious daughter,

In a world that constantly tries to define you, remember this: I have already defined who you are. You are Mine, cherished and chosen, treasured beyond measure.

You are part of My chosen family. You belong to Me in a special way, and I've set you apart as My treasured possession.

You are so precious to Me that I gave My life for you. That's how much you matter. I would do it all again, just for you. So, when doubts creep in and you question your value, remember the price I paid for you.

Every detail of who you are brings Me joy. I see the way you light up when you laugh. I notice how your heart aches to help others. I delight in the quirks and qualities that make you uniquely you.

You may feel pressure to fit in, to be like everyone else. But I created you to stand out, to shine with the unique light I've placed within you.

When you're scrolling through social media or comparing yourself to others, remember: you don't need to be like anyone else. You are perfectly loved, just as you are.

Your worth doesn't come from your achievements, your appearance, or what others think of you. It comes from My love for you.

So, today, and every day, hold your head high. You are My masterpiece, created with purpose and love.

Embrace your identity as My beloved daughter. Let this truth guide your actions, your words, and the way you see yourself.

In moments when you feel unlovable or unseen, come back to this truth: You are loved. You are valued. You are Mine.

And nothing can ever change that.

2
YOU ARE SAFE

My beautiful child,

I see the worries that sometimes cloud your mind. The butterflies in your stomach before a big test, the thoughts that race through your mind when you're lying in bed, the fear of what others might think of you.

I want you to know that I understand. You don't have to carry these burdens alone - just throw them all onto My strong shoulders. I'm not just willing to carry them; I'm eager to, because I love you so much.

You might feel pressure to be perfect, to do everything right. But I don't expect perfection from you. I love you just as you are. My power is made perfect in weakness (2 Corinthians 12:9), so it's okay to feel afraid or unsure sometimes. You don't have to be strong all the time.

Sometimes worry or stress can feel like a storm inside you that won't calm down. But remember, I am with you in the storm.

When the disciples were afraid in the boat during a tempest, I spoke "Peace, be still" to their storm. I calmed the winds and waves. I have the same power over the storms in your heart and mind.

My precious girl, don't be afraid, because I am right here with you. I'm your loving Heavenly Father. I'll give you strength. I'll help you. I'll hold you steady, keeping a firm grip on you with my strong hand (Isaiah 41:10). I won't let you go.

When worry feels big inside you, let me comfort you. My comfort can bring peace, and even joy, in the midst of your storms. (Psalm 94:19)

So, when anxious thoughts come, take a deep breath and remember that I am with you. You can talk to me anytime, anywhere. Tell me all your troubles, for I am your safe place (Psalm 62:8).

My peace is always available to you (John 14:27). And the peace I give is a gift the world cannot give. It's a peace of mind and heart. So don't be troubled or afraid. I am here, always ready to comfort you and bring you peace.

Let these promises sink deep into your heart.

Remember, the spirit I've given you isn't one of fear. It's one of power, love, and self-control. My power in you means that you're stronger than you know, braver than you believe, and more loved than you can possibly imagine. (2 Timothy 1:7)

I am always there when you're in trouble, providing a safe place and giving you the strength you need for each day. Trust in me, and let my peace, which transcends human understanding, guard your heart and mind (Philippians 4:7).

No matter what happens, you are always safe with me. I'm holding you in the palm of my hand.

3
YOU BELONG

My beloved daughter

I see your heart. I know how much you want to fit in, to have friends who truly understand you. Yet, sometimes you can feel lonely or left out, wondering if anyone really gets you. I want you to know that I understand completely. I am close to those whose hearts are hurting (Psalm 34:18), and I'm right there with you in those moments.

It's okay to feel uncertain about friendships. Making friends and keeping them isn't always easy. You might worry about saying the wrong thing or not being cool enough. But remember, I have made you wonderfully complex (Psalm 139:14). Your uniqueness is not a flaw—it's a gift.

When you're with your friends, you don't have to pretend to be someone you're not. I love you exactly as you are, and true friends will too. Don't be afraid to be yourself. A real friend will love you no matter what (Proverbs 17:17), on your good days and your not-so-good days.

If you're struggling to find your place, know that I have good plans for you (Jeremiah 29:11). Those plans include meaningful friendships. Keep your heart open. Be kind to others, even when it's hard. Your kindness might be exactly what someone else needs.

Remember that, whatever happens, you always have a friend in Me. I've called you friend (John 15:15), and I invite you to walk closely with Me every day. Talk to Me about anything and everything – your joys, your worries, your questions. I'm always listening out for your voice, longing to hear your thoughts.

Let Me guide your steps as you go through each day. When you spend time with Me – reading My words, talking to Me in prayer – you'll find a friendship deeper than any other.

Walking with Me doesn't mean you won't need other friends. But it does mean you can never be alone. I am your constant companion, in every hallway, at every lunch table, during every late-night worry. Let My presence give you confidence as you navigate your other friendships.

The same hands that set the stars in place are holding your heart, and I'm weaving connections and friendships into your story that will unfold in my perfect timing.

You belong, my child. You belong to Me, and you have a place in this world.

In the moments when friendship feels complicated, or loneliness tries to whisper lies about your worth, hold onto this truth: I chose you. I delight in you.

You are never too much, never too little, never too different, never too ordinary. You are exactly who I created you to be. And that, my precious child, is more than enough.

Rest in that truth today, tomorrow, and always.

4
YOU ARE BEAUTIFUL

My precious daughter,

I see you looking in the mirror. I hear the whispers in your heart when you compare yourself to others. Let me tell you a secret: you are beautifully and wonderfully made. I created every part of you with purpose and love. (Psalm 139:14)

True beauty comes from who you are inside – your kindness, your courage, your loving heart. These are the things that truly matter to me. (1 Samuel 16:7)

I know it can be hard when the world seems to focus so much on how you look. But remember, your worth isn't found in your appearance or in fitting into who or what others think you should be.

I look at your heart. The real you – the you that I see – is so much more than what's on the outside. You are my masterpiece, created to do amazing things that I planned long ago. (Ephesians 2:10)

I've given you unique gifts to fulfill that purpose. You might not see all of these gifts yet, but I do. I see the strength in you, the creativity, the kindness, the potential to change the world in your own special way.

When you think about your body, remember that I live within you. Your body is precious because it houses your beautiful spirit, and it allows you to do wonderful things in this world. Treat it with kindness and respect. (1 Corinthians 6:19-20)

Don't let the world's ever-changing ideas of beauty make you doubt yourself. I've given you your own unique beauty. Embrace it.

Remember, I don't make mistakes. Every freckle, every curve, every part of you was crafted with love. You don't need to change to be loved or accepted by me. I love you just as you are, right now, in this moment.

Remember, I don't make ordinary things – everything I create is extraordinary, including you. So when you look in the mirror, don't just see your outward appearance. See yourself through my eyes.

See the beautiful heart I've given you, the mind I've gifted you with, the unique abilities I've placed within you. You are fearfully and wonderfully made, inside and out. (Psalm 139:14)

When doubts creep in, hold onto this truth: you are my beloved child. I delight in you. I rejoice over you. (Zephaniah 3:17)

The beauty I see in you is so much more than any mirror shows - it's in your kind heart, your brave spirit, your way of seeing the world, and in every feature I carefully crafted.

You are my masterpiece and you are beautiful, inside and out.

5
YOU ARE CREATED FOR JOY

My cherished child,

I want you to know the real joy that comes from living in My presence. It's a joy that goes beyond your circumstances, a joy that flows from My Spirit living in you. (Galatians 5:22)

In a world that often focuses on big, exciting events, I invite you to find joy in the everyday moments. Each small moment is a gift from My hand, little love notes to brighten your day.

You see, I am always with you, in every moment. And where I am, there is fullness of joy. (Psalm 16:11) When you learn to recognise My presence in the ordinary, your whole life becomes an adventure of joy.

My Spirit lives within you, ready to guide you into this life of joy. He will teach you to see the world through My eyes, to find the beauty and goodness that I've woven into each day. As you follow His leading, you'll discover a deep well of joy that never runs dry.

This doesn't mean every moment will be happy or easy. But even in the midst of challenges, My joy can be your strength.

(Nehemiah 8:10) It's a joy that comes from knowing you are deeply loved, completely forgiven, and never alone.

When you wake up each morning, take a moment to invite My Spirit to fill you afresh. Ask Him to open your eyes to the good things around you, to guide your steps and your choices.

Look for Me in the little things each day. Pause to appreciate a flower, savour a meal, or enjoy the feeling of a job well done. These are all gifts from Me, opportunities to experience My joy.

Did you know that the more you practice joy, the easier it becomes? Even on the hard days, you can choose joy. The more you choose joy, the easier it will become to make that choice.

Remember, I delight in you, My precious girl. I love to see you smiling, laughing, enjoying the life I've given you. You bring Me so much joy, just by being you.

My joy is always within reach, because I am always within you. It's not something you have to strive for or earn. It's a gift, freely given, flowing from My heart to yours.

As you go through your day, keep your heart open to My Spirit's whispers. He will point out moments of joy you might have missed, little glimpses of My grace and love. Follow His lead, and watch as your life becomes more joyful and complete.

So today, choose joy. Embrace each precious moment. Sing, dance, laugh, celebrate and create, knowing that I am with you. Let this truth sink deep into your heart: You were created for joy.

Let My joy be your secret strength, your inner light. No matter what the day brings, carry this treasure inside you - the unshakable, unstoppable, overflowing joy of My Spirit.

Rest in this truth, My child: You were created for joy. It's not just something you feel; it's who you are in Me. So live joyfully today, shining My light wherever you go.

6
YOU ARE STRONG

My brave child,

Sometimes it feels like everyone wants you to be just like them, doesn't it? But I want you to know something amazing: I made you to be uniquely you!

When your friends are doing something that doesn't feel right, remember that you have a special strength inside you. This strength comes from Me, and it's always there, even when you feel unsure. For I can do everything through Christ, who gives me strength. (Philippians 4:13 NLT)

Being different can feel scary sometimes. But guess what? You're not alone. I'm right here with you, cheering you on! I've given you a spirit of power, love, and self-discipline. (2 Timothy 1:7 NLT) That means you have the power to make good choices, even when it's hard.

Your true friends will like you for who you are, not for who they want you to be. And when you stay true to yourself and to Me, you might be surprised – you could inspire others to do the right thing too! Don't let anyone think less of you because you are young. Be an example to all believers in what you say, in the way you live, in your love, your faith, and your purity. (1 Timothy 4:12 NLT)

When you feel pressured, remember that no temptation has overtaken you except what is common to mankind. And I am faithful; I will not let you be tempted beyond what you can bear. But when you are tempted, I will also provide a way out so that you can endure it. (1 Corinthians 10:13)

You can always talk to Me about these tough situations. If you need wisdom, just ask Me, and I'll generously give it to you. (James 1:5 NLT) I'm always here to listen and guide you, for I am your shepherd. (Psalm 23:1)

You are strong, My child. Not because you never feel pressure, but because you have the courage to be yourself – the wonderful person I created you to be. Don't copy the behaviour and customs of this world, but let Me transform you into a new person by changing the way you think. (Romans 12:2 NLT)

Keep shining your unique light. You never know who might need to see it! What's one way you can be true to yourself today?

7
YOU ARE MINDFUL

My precious daughter,

You were created for a life of peace and simplicity.

I know that the constant stream of information and opinions can be overwhelming. When the noise of the world feels too loud, turn to Me. When you need wisdom to navigate this complex world, turn to Me. (James 1:5 NLT) I'm always here to help you.

When negative influences try to infiltrate your thoughts, remember who you are in Me. You are My precious child, and no one can snatch you away from Me. (John 10:28 NLT) Don't let anyone's hurtful or unkind words define you.

When the online world feels overwhelming, remember that I offer you a peace that goes beyond anything you can understand. And this peace will guard your hearts and minds as you live in Christ Jesus. (Philippians 4:7 NLT) This peace is always available to you, even when your notifications are going crazy!

When you feel anxious about what's happening online, take a deep breath and remember: You can do everything through Me. I will give you strength. (Philippians 4:13 NLT) This strength includes finding calm in the midst of a busy digital world.

Find moments of quiet to be still and know that I am God. (Psalm 46:10 NLT) Give your mind regular breaks from technology. In these quiet times, I can renew your mind and bring you peace.

I've given you a spirit of power, love, and self-discipline (2 Timothy 1:7 NLT), and this includes the power and wisdom to know when to unplug from the stress of social media and find quiet in your mind.

Your mind is precious to Me, and I want you to experience the joy and peace that comes from focusing on good things. So keep thinking about things that are excellent and worthy of praise. (Philippians 4:8 NLT) This will help you find balance and happiness, both online and off.

Use your mind to spread positivity. Encourage each other and build each other up. (1 Thessalonians 5:11 NLT) Your kind words can make a big difference in someone's day and thoughts.

You are so much more than your likes, followers, or online presence. You are My beloved child, and nothing in the digital world can change that. Rest in this truth, and let it bring peace to your heart and mind.

8
YOU ARE GIFTED

My beloved daughter,

I want you to know that you are wonderfully made, with a special purpose in mind. Long before you were born, I had amazing plans for you. (Jeremiah 1:5 NLT)

I've given you special gifts (1 Peter 4:10 NLT). These gifts aren't just talents like singing or drawing - they include things like kindness, leadership, or being a good listener.

Everyone has different gifts (Romans 12:6 NLT). You might wonder what you're good at or what you're meant to do. Don't worry if you haven't figured out all your gifts yet. Part of the excitement is discovering them!

Take time to try new things. Pay attention to what brings you joy. Listen to what others appreciate about you. Your special qualities are part of My plan.

Your purpose isn't so much about what you do, but about who you are becoming. I want you to grow to be more like Jesus.

Sometimes, you might feel pressure to be like everyone else. But remember, I made you unique for a reason. Don't copy the behavior and customs of this world, but let me transform you into a new person by changing the way you think. (Romans 12:2)

When you're not sure what to do or which way to turn, don't forget that you can always come to Me. I'm here, ready to listen and guide you. You don't need to have all the answers – that's My job!

If you're feeling confused about your gifts or your purpose, just ask Me. I love it when you come to Me with your questions and uncertainties. I'll never get upset with you for asking (James 1:5 NLT). Instead, I'll generously share My wisdom with you.

I'm always here, eager to help you understand the special qualities I've given you and the amazing plans I have for your life.

Using your talents to help others is a wonderful way to show My love. (1 Peter 4:10) When you do this, you're not just making others happy - you're bringing Me joy too!

Remember, discovering your purpose is a journey. You don't have to have it all figured out right now.

I know the plans I have for you. They are plans for good and not for disaster, to give you a future and a hope. (Jeremiah 29:11 NLT)

You are unique. Your gifts and talents are a reflection of My creativity. As you grow and learn, keep your heart open to the ways I'm working in and through you.

Trust in Me, and don't be afraid to shine brightly with the gifts I've given you. You are loved, you are valued, and you have an important part to play in this world.

Rest in that truth today, and be excited about the purpose I have for you!

9
YOU ARE A TRUTH-BEARER

My cherished child,

The truth will set you free. This isn't just a saying—it's My promise to you. When you live honestly, you'll find a freedom that nothing else can give you.

I am the God of truth. Every word I speak is true and trustworthy. When I make a promise, I always keep it. You can count on My words because I cannot lie.

Just as I am truthful, I've created you to be a bearer of truth in this world. When you see something wrong happening - to you or to someone else - try to find your voice, even if it feels scary to do so.

When you speak honestly and live with integrity, you reflect My character. You become like a bright light in a sometimes dark world.

Remember, your words have power. They can bring life and healing, or they can hurt. That's why I encourage you to speak the truth in love. When you do this, you help others grow and you grow too.

Living truthfully isn't always easy. In those moments, remember that I see everything and I'm always here to help you choose what's right. Remember that courage isn't the absence of fear - it's doing what's right even when you're afraid. My strength is available to you whenever you need it.

I've given you a spirit of power, love, and self-discipline. This includes the power to be honest, even when it's hard. You can always pray to Me for help to speak and live truthfully.

Being honest and having integrity might not always make you popular, but it will make you trustworthy. And trust is a precious gift you can give to others.

When you make a mistake—and everyone does sometimes—be quick to admit it. There's freedom in confessing the truth and asking for forgiveness. I'm always ready to forgive you, and I'll help you make things right with others too.

Remember, you're My precious child. I've given you the ability to make good choices. When you're not sure what to do, just ask Me. I'm always here to guide you and help you choose the path of truth.

Your voice matters. Your perspective matters. When you speak up with kindness and courage, when you stand up for those who can't stand up for themselves, you can create change.

Remember, you are created in My image. I've put My truth inside you. Keep shining your light of truth in the world, My dear one. Your honesty can change lives and make the world a better place.

I believe in you, My little truth-bearer. Keep holding fast to what is true, noble, right, and pure. As you do, you'll grow strong in character and close to My heart.

10
YOU ARE CREATIVE

My precious daughter,

In the very first words of the Bible - "*In the beginning, God created...*" - I revealed my creative heart. I delight in creativity.

I created the world to be filled with beauty and joy. Think about the books you love, the music that moves you, and the art that touches your soul. All of these came about because someone dared to create. Each creative act adds something beautiful to the world. And you, my precious daughter, have your own unique beauty to bring forth.

True creativity isn't just about art or music or what the world might label as "creative." It's about bringing something new into the world - something that didn't exist before.

When you plan a surprise for a friend, find a solution to a problem, or even organise your room in a new way - that's creativity flowing through you. Every time you dream a new dream or imagine new possibilities - you're reflecting My creative nature.

Maybe you don't feel creative. Perhaps you've been told you're "not the creative type" or "not artistic." But their words don't define you, I do.

Those negative words? They're like chains falling away as you embrace the truth of who you really are - My creative daughter, made in My image. Don't let fear or past hurts hold you back from exploring the creative gifts I've placed within you.

I've given you your own unique ways to create and express yourself. You don't have to be like anyone else or meet someone else's definition of "creative." Your creativity is as unique as your fingerprint - a special part of who I made you to be.

Embrace your unique gifts, even when others don't understand. Pursue your passions with courage, knowing that your uniqueness is your greatest strength.

Remember, I don't make mistakes. The creative spark inside you is there for a reason. It's not about being "the best" or comparing yourself to others. It's about embracing the joy of creating and letting your light shine in ways that only you can.

Those creative dreams stirring in your heart? I put them there. That desire to make something beautiful or meaningful? That comes from Me.

So take those small creative steps that call to your heart. Try new things. Express yourself. Don't be afraid to make mistakes - they're part of the creative journey.

I delight in watching you discover and develop the creative gifts I've given you. When you create, you reflect something of My nature to the world.

You are My child, My creativity lives in you. You are a masterpiece in progress. Let your creativity flow freely, knowing it comes from Me.

11
YOU ARE KIND

My dear child,

I've given you a special gift – a heart that cares deeply for others. This gift is called kindness, and it's a beautiful reflection of who I am. I am rich in kindness, tolerance, and patience. (Romans 2:4)

When you see someone hurting and you feel a tug in your heart to help, that's kindness. It's your heart reaching out to someone else's pain or struggle. This feeling is precious to me because it shows you're becoming more like me.

Sometimes, being kind might make you feel sad or even overwhelmed. That's okay. Jesus, too, was moved by the struggles he saw. When he saw the crowds, he had compassion on them, because they were troubled and helpless, like sheep without a shepherd. (Matthew 9:36)

Your kind heart might make you feel things more strongly than others. You might want to cry when you see someone else cry, or feel upset when you hear about someone being treated unfairly. Don't be ashamed of these feelings. They're a sign that you have a tender heart, just like I do.

Remember, I've chosen you to be my very own. So clothe yourselves with tenderhearted mercy, kindness, humility, gentleness, and patience. (Colossians 3:12) These qualities start in your heart, and your kindness helps them grow.

There might be times when you feel like you can't fix the big problems you see. That's alright. Kindness isn't about fixing everything; it's about caring. Even when you can't change a situation, your kind heart can make a difference just by caring.

Your kind heart might sometimes make you feel different from others. Some people might not understand why you care so much. But I want you to know that this sensitivity is a strength, not a weakness. It's a part of who I created you to be.

As you grow, your kindness will grow too. You'll learn how to balance caring deeply with taking care of yourself. Remember, Jesus often took time alone to rest and pray. It's okay for you to do the same when your heart feels heavy.

Always remember, your kind heart is a gift. Your kindness isn't weakness; it's strength. It allows you to love others the way I love them. And as you show kindness, you'll understand my love for you even more. Love each other in the same way I have loved you. (John 13:34)

You have been give a soft and tender heart, my child. Cherish this gift, protect this softness, and watch how it becomes a force more powerful than any hardness the world can throw at you.

Your kind heart is My love made visible.

12
YOU ARE BRAVE

My precious child,

In the storms of life, you may wonder where to find strength. Sometimes, when the path ahead seems dark and uncertain, you may wonder if your faith is strong enough.

Even when your faith feels small, remember that I can use it in mighty ways. When the disciples faced a storm, Jesus used their tiny faith to accomplish great things. You don't need huge faith - you just need to place your small faith in Me. If you have faith as small as a mustard seed, nothing will be impossible for you. (Matthew 17:20)

When you feel weak, remember this: My strength lives in you. So, be strong and courageous. Do not be afraid... for I go with you; I will never leave you nor forsake you. (Deuteronomy 31:6)

When doubts creep in or when circumstances feel overwhelming, remember that I am holding you. This is exactly when My strength can shine brightest. My power works best in weakness. (2 Corinthians 12:9) Your bravery isn't about feeling fearless - it's about trusting Me even when you're afraid.

You might think others are braver than you, but true courage often looks like taking one small step while your heart is pounding. It's okay to feel scared. Even great heroes of faith had moments of fear. But they kept their eyes on Me, and I carried them through. I will do the same for you.

Remember what I've brought you through before. Each time you've trusted Me through hard times, your faith has grown stronger. These challenges aren't easy, but they're helping you develop a deeper trust in Me.

In difficult times, you don't have to pretend to be strong. Come to Me with your fears, your tears, your questions. Pour out your heart to Me. I am your safe place, your refuge, your strength in times of trouble.

Remember, you are brave because you know Who holds you even in your fear. You are brave because I live in you. My Spirit gives you strength beyond your own (2 Timothy 1:7).

Trust in My love today. Let my strength be your courage. Remember, you don't walk this path alone - I am right here with you, every step of the way.

13
YOU ARE HELD

My beloved child,

I have good plans for you – plans for good and not for disaster, to give you a future and a hope. (Jeremiah 29:11) Just because things didn't work out the way you expected doesn't mean they won't work out at all. I see the bigger picture, and I'm always working things out for your good.

I know there are times when things don't go the way you hoped, but I want you to remember something important: you are never alone in any situation. I am holding you through every moment. My arms are always around you, ready to comfort and strengthen you.

When you're feeling disappointed or let down, rest in My embrace. Pour out your heart to Me, make me your refuge. (Psalm 62:8) You can tell Me anything – your frustrations, your sadness, your anger. I can hold all of your feelings.

Even in your darkest moments, remember that I can turn what seems bad into something good. What others might intend to harm you, I can use for good. (Genesis 50:20) This is a promise you can hold onto when life feels overwhelming.

It's okay to feel sad when you're disappointed. When your heart hurts, know that I am close.

No matter what's happening, try to find something to be thankful for. (1 Thessalonians 5:18) This doesn't mean you have to be happy about difficult situations, but it's an invitation to find something to be thankful for.

Life can sometimes feel like a rollercoaster, with ups and downs you didn't expect. I see it all. I hold it all. I care for you deeply.

When tough times come, remember that you're not alone. Rest in My embrace. My love for you is like a strong anchor, keeping you steady even when things feel shaky. Nothing will ever be able to separate you from my love (Romans 8:39).

When you trust in Me, you'll find a new strength within you. You'll soar high above your troubles, just like an eagle. You'll run towards your goals without getting tired, and you'll walk through challenges without giving up. (Isaiah 40:31)

Sometimes, difficult experiences are a chance for you to grow and learn. They can teach you patience, perseverance, and how to trust Me more.

My child, I've put My strength inside you. So when you feel disappointed, take a deep breath, remember how much I love you, and trust me for the strength and patience you need.

Always remember, you are precious to me. You are safe in My arms, my child. Nothing can ever change that.

You are held, My precious child - today, tomorrow, and always.

14
YOU ARE ACCEPTED

My precious daughter,

Making mistakes is part of life. But your mistakes don't define you.

Everyone messes up. Everyone. The difference is how you respond to those moments. My love doesn't keep score. It doesn't hold onto your mistakes or use them to make you feel small. Instead, My love is like a gentle hand that helps you back up, dusts you off, and says, "Let's try again."

When shame whispers lies, like 'You're not good enough", remember I paid an incredible price to restore you. Not because you earned it, but because you are precious to Me. I gave my life for you, so that you could be fully accepted into my family (John 3:16).

I want you to know that my grace is bigger than your biggest mistake. My love is stronger than your failures.

Grace gives you a second chance, even when you don't think you deserve it. It's like getting a free pass, not because you earned it, but because I love you that much.

Grace is a gift, freely given to you. You don't have to earn it or deserve it. It's yours because of my great love for you (Ephesians 2:8-9). I love you so much that I'm willing to forgive you and give you another shot, even when you mess up.

Grace isn't about getting away with things. It isn't about pretending you didn't mess up. It's about understanding that your worth isn't determined by how well you do or don't do, but by My unconditional love.

Grace doesn't ignore your mistakes - it covers them completely. It doesn't just hide them; it transforms them. Every mistake, every moment of shame - is covered. Think of it like a reset button that wipes away the guilt and gives you hope.

The world will tell you that you need to earn your worth. That you must be perfect to be loved. But you are loved exactly where you are, precisely as you are. My love doesn't wait for you to get it all right. My love is what helps you become more.

Sometimes the hardest person to forgive is yourself. You replay your mistakes like a movie that won't stop playing.

Forgiving yourself isn't weakness. It's not the easy option. It takes courage and strength to look at your mistakes, acknowledge them, and then choose to believe that they don't define you.

My child, you are not the times you've messed up or made mistakes. You are My beloved daughter, crafted with purpose, loved without condition.

So, forgive yourself. Speak kindly to yourself. Treat yourself with love and compassion. Accept yourself. Just as I accept you.

You are loved and accepted. Completely. Unconditionally. Eternally.

Rest in that truth.

15
YOU ARE UNSTOPPABLE

My courageous daughter,

I know life can sometimes make you feel small or insignificant. The world might try to limit you with labels or low expectations. But I want you to know that My power in you is boundless. I am able to do immeasurably more than you could ever ask or imagine, according to My power that is at work within you. (Ephesians 3:20)

Did you know that the same power that raised Jesus from the grave lives inside you? (Ephesians 1:19-20) That's right - if you have accepted Me into your heart, you have resurrection power flowing through your veins!

This power is greater than any force in the universe. No problem, no enemy, no challenge can stand against the incredible power of My Spirit within you. (Romans 8:31)

Jesus demonstrated this unstoppable power when He healed the sick, calmed storms, and raised the dead. And He promised that you would do even greater things than He did, because He was going to the Father. (John 14:12) That's the kind of power you have access to!

So when you face obstacles that seem too big, when you're up against circumstances that appear hopeless, remember the death-defying power that resides in you. Believe that I can do the impossible in and through you.

My child, the enemy may try to discourage you, to make you doubt your strength. But always remember: the One who is in you is greater than the one who is in the world. (1 John 4:4 NIV) No weapon turned against you will succeed. (Isaiah 54:17 NLT) With Me, you are unstoppable!

Remember, you are not fighting for victory; you are fighting from victory. I have already won the ultimate battle through My death and resurrection. You are on the winning side! So walk in the confidence of knowing that nothing can defeat you when you are in Me.

You are unstoppable, My child. Not because of your own might or abilities, but because of the mighty Spirit that lives within you. You have resurrection power, world-changing power, flowing through your being.

So rise up, daughter. Keep going forward in faith, knowing that with Me, all things are possible. (Matthew 19:26) Rise up in the power of My might. Let My strength be your confidence. You are unstoppable because My unstoppable power is in you.

16
YOU ARE PATIENT AND PERSISTENT

My precious child,

I know that sometimes it can be hard to wait - for dreams to unfold, for prayers to be answered, for changes to come.

In a world of instant everything, patience can feel like a lost art. But waiting is not just about passing time - it's about growing stronger.

Think of how a tiny seed waits patiently in the dark soil before it breaks through to the sunlight. Each day underground isn't wasted - it's growing stronger roots. That's what patience does in your life too.

When you feel like giving up, when things take longer than you hoped or when your prayers don't seem to be answered right away, remember, My precious daughter, that waiting time is never wasted time. These moments of patience are My preparation time. I'm working behind the scenes in ways you can't see yet, orchestrating everything for your good, helping you grow stronger. Even when it feels like nothing is happening, I am preparing you for something beautiful.

When your prayers seem to go unanswered, trust that I am working even when you can't see it. When you face difficult times, - those days that test your faith and challenge your heart - know that each trial you face is helping you grow stronger, teaching you to persevere. I'm using every situation, even the tough ones, to shape you into everything I've created you to be, complete and lacking nothing.

Patience isn't about gritting your teeth or white-knuckling it through - it's about trusting My timing. I have made everything beautiful in its time. (Ecclesiastes 3:11) Just as a skilled potter knows exactly how long to leave the clay on the wheel, I know exactly how long to let circumstances shape you.

In those moments when waiting feels unbearable, lean into My strength. The fruit of My Spirit living in you includes patience. (Galatians 5:22) This means you don't have to manufacture patience on your own - it grows naturally as you stay connected to Me.

Remember that patience isn't weakness - it's quiet strength. Put your hope in Me. Every time you choose to trust My timing instead of rushing ahead, you'll grow stronger. Every time you persevere through a difficult season, you're growing a little more like Me.

I notice your faithfulness in the small things - when you keep trying even when things are hard, when you keep hoping even though the answer hasn't come yet.

Be patient, My child. Allow My Spirit to work in you, teaching you to trust My perfect timing. Let patient strength grow in you day by day, knowing that I am faithful to complete the good work I've begun in you.

Take heart, beloved. Your patient endurance is creating something beautiful in you - faith that will carry you through any storm and strength that will last a lifetime.

17
YOU ARE GENEROUS

My treasured one,

I am a God Who loves to give, and I love to give to you, my child.

I want to tell you a beautiful truth about generosity: it's a reflection of My heart. When you live with a spirit of generosity, you are mirroring My character to the world.

Generosity is about so much more than money or possessions. It's about giving of yourself - your time, your talents, your presence, your heart. It's about showing up authentically and sharing the unique gifts I've given you.

When you give your genuine smile, your listening ear, your compassionate words, you are offering priceless presents that can change someone's life.

I know that being generous can sometimes feel risky. You might wonder if you'll have enough time, enough energy, enough resources for yourself if you give to others.

But when you give back to Me, when you trust Me with your resources and your heart, I will pour out blessings in your life

(Malachi 3:10). Not just material blessings, but blessings of joy, peace, purpose, and provision. You can never outgive Me!

Being generous takes an act of faith. It's believing that I will take care of you as you care for others. It's trusting that I have given you everything you need to make a difference, and that as you pour out, I will keep filling you up.

I delight in generosity, My daughter. It brings Me great joy to see you sharing My love and My blessings with the world.

So keep giving from the overflow of who I've made you to be, My precious girl and watch as I throw open the doors of heaven and shower you with blessing.

When you give from the overflow of what I've given you, you are showing the world a glimpse of My generous heart. Keep looking for opportunities to give - of your presence, to share your story, to extend compassion - to be genuinely, generously you.

I love you with an unstoppable, generous love. And it's this never-ending love that empowers you to live with open hands and an open heart. So, give with joy, give with faith, give with the confidence that I will always provide what you need.

And always remember, My daughter: your generous heart, your authentic spirit, your unique presence - these are all gifts that the world needs. As you give of yourself, you are not just making a difference; you are being the difference.

So keep shining, keep giving, keep pouring out the love and light I've put within you. The world is better because you are in it, and your generosity is a powerful force for good.

And I will be with you every step of the way, cheering you on, filling you up, and delighting in the beautiful ways you reflect My heart. Keep being the gift you are, My precious girl. This world needs you!

18
YOU ARE KNOWN

My precious daughter,

Long before you took your first breath, I knew you. Before you were even a thought in your parents' minds, you were a dream in My heart. I knew you before I formed you in the womb (Jeremiah 1:5).

Yes! The God of the universe, the One who painted the sunsets and scattered the stars, knew you intimately before you were even born. I've known every detail of your life from the very beginning.

I know everything about you. I know the number of hairs on your head (Luke 12:7). I know your favourite colour and the song that makes you want to dance. I know your hopes and your fears, your strengths and your struggles. There's not a single part of you that is hidden from Me.

But here's what might surprise you: knowing everything about you only makes Me love you more. My love for you isn't based on your performance or your perfection. It's based on who I am and who I've created you to be.

I know the plans I have for you (Jeremiah 29:11). Plans to give you hope and a future. Plans to use every part of your story for something beautiful. Even the chapters that feel messy or painful - I can weave those into a story of redemption.

When you feel misunderstood or alone, remember that I see you. I get you. I understand every part of your heart, even the parts you hide from everyone else. You are fully known and fully loved by Me.

On the days when you doubt yourself, when you question your worth or your purpose, come back to this truth: the One who knows you best loves you most. My love for you is not based on what you do, but on who you are - My precious, irreplaceable daughter.

I am with you in every moment, in every season. I know your past, your present, and your future. And in all of it, My love for you never changes. It's a love that's stronger than your deepest fear, bigger than your biggest mistake, and more constant than the rising sun.

So today, rest in the beautiful truth that you are known - wholly, completely, intimately known by the God who loves you without limits. Let this knowledge fill you with peace, with joy, with the unshakable confidence of a girl who knows she is forever cherished.

Find freedom and joy in the freedom of being fully seen and fully loved. Find peace and acceptance in being known by the King of Kings. And walk forward in the adventure of life, hand in hand with the God who will never let you go.

You are known, precious daughter. Every part of you. And you are deeply, fiercely, eternally loved. Always remember that.

19
YOU ARE PRECIOUS

My precious daughter,

Do you know how precious and valuable you are to Me? I want you to understand a life-changing truth today: your worth is not based on anything the world values. It's not about your grades, your appearance, your popularity, or your performance. Your value comes from My great love for you.

You see, I love you so deeply that I was willing to pay the highest price to make you My own. I gave My only Son to bring you into My family forever. That's how much you mean to Me. That's how valuable you are in My eyes.

The world might try to put price tags on your worth based on all kinds of superficial things. But I want you to see yourself the way I see you -- as a rare and priceless treasure.

When you understand your true value, it changes everything. You don't have to chase after the approval of others because you already have My unconditional love. You don't need to compare yourself to anyone else because you are uniquely designed by Me. You can walk with confidence, knowing that the King of the universe calls you His cherished daughter.

I know there might be days when you don't feel valuable. You might feel overlooked, unappreciated, or even worthless. But those feelings don't change the facts of how precious you are to Me. In those moments, remember the cross -- the ultimate display of your worth to Me.

I loved you so much that I gave up my only Son for you. I paid the highest price to make you my own (1 Corinthians 6:20). You are more valuable than gold, silver, or diamonds. Your worth is based on my lavish, sacrificial, never-stopping love. And nothing can ever change that.

When you start to see your worth through My eyes, you'll find a new freedom. My love isn't something you have to work for; it's a gift that's freely given to you. Instead of striving to earn love or prove your value, you can rest in the truth that you are loved and treasured.

So hold your head high today, My daughter. Walk tall. You are precious and treasured by the King. You are valuable, not by the world's ever-changing standards, but by the unchanging reality of My love for you.

Carry this truth with you wherever you go. Let it shape the way you think about yourself and others. When you know your true worth, you'll be free to live with joy, confidence, and purpose.

You are a priceless masterpiece, an irreplaceable treasure. And nothing will ever change that. I am with you always, celebrating the precious value I've placed within you.

20
YOU ARE FORGIVEN

My precious child,

I see the hurt in your heart. The pain caused by others can feel overwhelming. But in Me, you can find the strength to forgive. While you were still a sinner, I demonstrated My love for you by sending Christ to die for you. (Romans 5:8)

My forgiveness for you is complete, unconditional, and eternal. When you came to Me, I forgave all your sins—past, present, and future. I removed them as far as the east is from the west. (Psalm 103:12) Isn't that amazing? No matter what you've done, My forgiveness is always available. All you need to do is ask, and I will cleanse you from all unrighteousness. (1 John 1:9)

I know that forgiving others isn't easy—but it's the path to freedom and joy. When you choose to forgive, you're reflecting My character to the world. You're showing others what My love looks like in action.

Don't be discouraged if forgiveness doesn't come instantly. It's a journey we'll take together. You might need to forgive seventy times seven—just as I forgive you. (Matthew 18:22) I'm right here, helping you with each step.

Forgiving doesn't mean forgetting or pretending the hurt didn't happen. It means choosing to release the offender from the debt they owe you, just as I've cancelled your debt. (Colossians 2:14) Remember that I've forgiven you everything. Let that help you to forgive others.

When forgiveness feels impossible, lean on Me. My grace is sufficient for you, and My power is made perfect in your weakness. (2 Corinthians 12:9) Let My love flow through you, bringing healing to your heart and touching the lives of those around you.

As you forgive, you're participating in My kingdom work. You're breaking the cycle of bitterness and spreading My peace. This is how you can be My peacemaker in a world full of conflict. (Matthew 5:9)

Remember, My child, you are forgiven. Let this truth penetrate your heart: there is now no condemnation for those who are in Christ Jesus. (Romans 8:1) From this place of being fully forgiven, extend that same grace to others. Trust Me to guide you. I am with you always, empowering you to forgive as I have forgiven you.

21
YOU ARE CHOSEN

My treasured daughter,

You are chosen. Hand-picked. Selected. Set apart. Not because of anything you've done, but because of who I am and how much I love you.

Your existence is no accident. I chose and created you with great intention and love.

Long before you were born, I knew you. I formed you in your mother's womb with great care and purpose. I chose you to be My special treasure, My beloved child. (Psalm 139:13-16)

In a world that often measures worth by popularity, achievements, or appearance, remember that your value comes from Me. I don't choose based on outward qualities, but I look at the heart. (1 Samuel 16:7) And when I look at you, I see a masterpiece, created in My very own image. (Genesis 1:27)

You might wonder sometimes, "Why me?" You might feel uncertain of your place, your purpose. But I want you to know that I have a plan for you, a destiny that only you can fulfil. I've chosen you to be a part of My story, to make a difference in this broken world.

You are chosen. Not because you are perfect, but because you are perfectly loved. Rest in this identity, let it seep into every part of your being. It's the foundation on which you can build a life of purpose, joy, and unshakable peace.

My choice is not based on your strength, your wisdom, or your perfection. In fact, I often choose those who the world might dismiss, to show My power and grace. (1 Corinthians 1:27-29)

When you feel weak, remember that I am strong. When you feel inadequate, remember that I am more than enough. I've chosen you not because you are perfect, but because I am perfect in you. My power shines brightest in your weakness. (2 Corinthians 12:9)

You are never alone. I am with you always, guiding your steps, leading you into the wonderful future I have planned for you. Trust in My choosing, even when the path seems unclear. I will direct your steps. (Proverbs 16:9)

Being chosen doesn't mean life will always be easy. There will be challenges, obstacles, moments of doubt. But in every situation, remember that I have chosen you, and I will always be by your side. Nothing can separate you from My love. (Romans 8:38-39)

So today, hold your head high. Walk in confidence, not in your own abilities, but in the unshakable truth of My choosing. You are wanted. You are valuable. You are destined for great things.

Embrace your identity as My chosen one. Let it be the lens through which you see yourself, the world, and your future. And know that as you journey through life, you do so as one who is dearly loved, handpicked, and forever Mine.

You are My chosen treasure, My precious daughter. Never forget how precious and valued you are.

22
YOU ARE ANCHORED

My beautiful child,

Sometimes the world feels peaceful and safe, but sometimes life can feel like a storm at sea – waves of change crash around you and the winds of uncertainty blow strong.

In these moments, I want you to remember one unchanging truth: I am your strong and unbreakable anchor. (Hebrews 6:19 TPT) You are anchored not by your own strength, but by Mine. I am the One who is holding on to you, just as the anchor holds a ship steady through the fiercest storm.

When everything around you seems to be changing, My love for you remains constant and unchanging through every season.

My beloved, I know that the waves of change can make your heart feel unsteady, like a small boat on choppy waters. But I am right here, holding you secure through every change.

In Me, you have a rock that cannot be shaken, a fortress that stands firm in every storm. (Psalm 62:6) When everything feels uncertain, let this truth anchor your heart: I am your unchanging rock, your safe harbour in the storm.

You can always pour out your heart to Me – your fears, your confusion, your questions about the future. And you know what? I love it when you do. (Psalm 62:8) You never have to pretend to be brave with Me. I'm strong enough to embrace all your feelings, all your fears, all your wonderings about what's ahead.

Remember that while circumstances change, I never do. I am the same yesterday, today, and forever. (Hebrews 13:8) You can count on My promises. You can trust in My faithfulness. You can anchor your heart in My unchanging love.

When you feel tossed or buffeted about by life's changes, draw near to Me. Find your safety in Me. Pour out your heart. (Psalm 62:8) Confide in me your fears and your worries about what's ahead. I am listening, and I understand.

Remember, being anchored in Me doesn't mean there won't be any storms. It means you have something stronger than the storms to hold onto. My love for you is deeper than any ocean, stronger than any wave of change that comes your way.

I am holding on to you. Like a mighty anchor that keeps a ship secure in the fiercest storm, My grip on you is strong and sure. You are anchored, My precious one – not because of your own strength, but because of Mine. Rest secure in this truth today.

23
YOU ARE PEACE-FILLED

My chosen child,

In a world that can sometimes feel chaotic and unpredictable, I want to remind that, in Me, you can always find peace. Not just any peace, but a perfect, unshakable peace that goes beyond what the human mind can understand. (Philippians 4:7)

You might look around and see a world filled with turmoil - conflicts, divisions, uncertainties. These challenges can make you feel anxious, afraid, and overwhelmed. But I want you to know that you don't have to face these storms alone. I am your anchor in the chaos and your safe harbour in the storm. (Isaiah 9:6)

When the world around you feels shaky, remember that I am your firm foundation. I never change. My love for you remains constant and unwavering, no matter what circumstances you face. You can build your life on the solid rock of My faithfulness. (Matthew 7:24-25)

When anxiety tries to take hold of your heart, come to Me. Tell Me your worries, your fears, your struggles. I care about every detail of your life. (1 Peter 5:7)

When you find yourself in a whirlwind of stress or worry, take a moment to pause. Breathe deeply. Tune your heart to the whispers of My Spirit. Remind yourself of My unchanging truths. Speak My promises over your situation. As you do, you'll feel My peace washing over you, stilling the storms inside your heart.

When you bring your burdens to Me in prayer, I will replace your anxiety with My peace. My peace is a supernatural gift that comes from My presence in your life.

Remember, peace isn't the absence of problems; it's the presence of My Spirit within you. As you learn to trust Me more, you'll find My peace guarding your heart and mind, even in the midst of life's storms. (Isaiah 26:3) When you focus on Me - My goodness, My faithfulness, My love for you - peace will begin to take root in your soul.

My precious one, I want you to know that the peace I give is a gift the world cannot give. So don't be troubled or afraid. (John 14:27) My peace is My gift to you, it comes from staying close to Me.

Even when the world feels out of control, remember that I am in control. I am with you always, holding you close to My heart. I am working all things together for your good, even when you can't see it. (Romans 8:28)

So keep coming back to Me, My daughter. Keep choosing to trust Me, even when it's hard. As you do, you'll find My peace becoming more and more your natural state of being - a peace that radiates from the inside out, touching not only your life but the lives of those around you.

You are precious to Me. You are loved. And in Me, you are always peaceful.

24
YOU ARE NOT ALONE

My precious daughter,

I see every tear you cry. Those quiet tears that fall when no one is looking. The ones that come from deep disappointment, from feeling misunderstood, from the ache of loss that seems too big for words.

You might feel confused, angry, or just deeply sad. Maybe you're wondering why things have to change, why people you care about can't stay the same.

Your heart might feel fragile, making it feel hard to even breathe Some days, getting out of bed might feel hard. Other days, you might feel angry or confused about why things are happening the way they are.

These feelings are real. They matter. And I want you to know - you are not alone in them. I am with you and will watch over you wherever you go. I will never leave you or forsake you.

I understand the jumble of emotions that can sweep over you - sadness one moment, anger the next, perhaps emptiness or loneliness. I see it all. I hold it all. I care for you.

When your heart hurts, I am close. Your big feelings don't overwhelm Me.

Come to me when you feel weary and burdened, and I will give your soul rest. I can handle everything you're experiencing, and I want to be your safe place in the midst of it.

When the pain feels too big, talk to Me. Pour out your heart just like you're reading this letter. You don't need fancy words. Just be honest. Tell Me exactly how you're feeling - the anger, the sadness, the confusion. I'm listening.

Find quiet moments to sit with Me. Maybe that's journaling, sitting outside, listening to worship music, or simply breathing deeply and knowing I'm near. You might not feel Me right away, and that's okay. I'm still here.

Ask Me to help you through this. And remember, healing takes time. Be gentle with yourself.

Some days may feel harder than others. Some moments might catch you by surprise, when a memory or a thought brings emotions rushing back. That's okay. Healing isn't a straight line. It's a journey, and I'm walking every step of it with you.

Remember, these feelings won't last forever. They don't define you. They're just visitors passing through your heart. And I am always here, steady and sure, waiting to comfort you.

You are loved. You are seen. You are not alone. And I am with you always, to the very end.

Rest in My arms, My precious child. I've got you.

25
YOU ARE PURE

My treasured child,

I want to talk to you about who you are in Me. Long before I created the world, I chose you to be set apart, precious and pure. (Ephesians 1:4) This isn't something you have to earn or achieve - it's already who you are because you belong to Me.

When you became My daughter, I made you new from the inside out. I placed My Spirit within you, making you pure and precious. Your body is not just yours, but a sacred space where I have chosen to make My home.

Think of it like this: a diamond is precious not because of what it does, but because of what it is. Its value doesn't come from what it does, but what it is. In the same way, you are precious to Me not because of what you do, but because of whose you are.

Being pure isn't a list of rules to follow, but a relationship to embrace. It's about walking with Me, letting My love reshape your heart. You don't have to 'try' to make yourself clean, I have already made you clean. Your holiness is a gift, not a goal.

I know the world tries to tell you that you need to be like everyone else. But I've made you different in the most beautiful way. Not different in a way that makes you uncomfortable or sets you apart awkwardly, but different because you shine with My light from the inside out.

My daughter, this isn't about trying to be good enough. You already are enough because My Spirit lives in you. Just as a spring naturally flows with pure water, My life naturally flows through you, making you shine with My light.

When you feel like you don't fit in, remember: you were never meant to. I created you to shine, to sparkle with My love in a way that only you can. My grace isn't just helping you - it's transforming you from the inside out.

Remember, precious one, your true identity comes from belonging to Me. You don't have to strive or struggle to be different - you already are, simply because you're Mine. Rest in this truth: I have made you new, pure, and precious, and nothing can change who you are in Me.

26
YOU ARE SPECIAL

My masterpiece,

Do you know how special you are to Me? You are Mine – chosen, cherished, and claimed as My very own. I want you to let that truth sink deep into your heart today: you are forever part of My family.

Before I formed you, I knew you. My hands shaped you with tender care, like a potter lovingly crafting His finest work. Every detail of who you are was thoughtfully created. You aren't a mistake or an accident – you are My masterpiece, carefully designed by My loving hands.

The world will often try to squeeze you into a mold, to make you conform, to convince you that fitting in is the goal. But I didn't create you to fit in. I created you to stand out, to shine in a way that only you can.

Your differences are not mistakes. They are not flaws to be corrected or smoothed away. They are beautiful brushstrokes in the masterpiece of who you are. That passion that keeps you up at night? Those seemingly random combination of interests? Those are whispers of the gifts I've placed inside you.

You see, I chose you. I adopted you into My royal family. You are now a daughter of the King, and nothing can ever change that status. This isn't something you earned or achieved; it's a gift of My love. I chose you simply because I love you.

When the world tries to tell you that you don't belong, remember this: you belong to Me. You are my daughter, adopted and accepted by Me.

You are irreplaceable. There has never been - and will never be - another you. The world needs exactly who you are, not a watered-down version of you trying to be like everyone else.

I have written your name on the palm of My hand. You are precious and honoured in My sight. Not because you're perfect – but because you're Mine.

Like a skilled potter, I am still at work in your life. Sometimes you might feel like you're being stretched or reshaped, and that's okay. Trust My hands. I know exactly what I'm doing, and I have wonderful plans for who you're becoming.

When you feel uncertain about who you are, come back to this truth: you are my precious child. Not because of anything you've done, but because of everything I've done for you. I paid the highest price to make you My own – the precious blood of My Son. That's how valuable you are to Me.

You don't have to strive to keep My love or earn My acceptance. You already have it. You don't have to worry about measuring up to others' expectations. You already delight My heart just by being who I created you to be.

Let this sink deep into your spirit: you are Mine. My treasured possession. My beloved daughter. My cherished creation.

No mistake you could make, no failure you might fear – nothing can separate you from My love or snatch you from My hand. You are Mine, and I am yours – forever.

27
YOU ARE NOBLE

My precious daughter,

You are the daughter of the King! You are royalty - not because of your grades, popularity, or achievements, but simply because you're Mine.

As My child, you're called to live differently. I know it's not always easy. Sometimes it might feel like people around you are not being true to themselves. You might wonder, "Does it really matter if I go along with the crowd?" But here's the thing: it does matter. Because every choice you make is shaping who you're becoming.

I've created you to be a girl who shines with truth and love, no matter what's going on around her. I've called you to be different, to stand out - not by being perfect, but by being real and authentic.

Being a child of the King isn't about status or perfection - it's about the posture of your heart. It's about approaching others with gentleness and humility, seeing them through My eyes.

When you walk in gentleness, you reflect My character. Gentleness isn't weakness - it's strength under control. Humility doesn't mean thinking less of yourself; it means recognising that every person you meet is valuable and worthy of respect. Gentleness and humility reveal my heart to a watching world.

Living as My daughter means living well, even when no one is watching. It's about seeing yourself and others through My eyes. It's about treating everyone with kindness and dignity, because they're precious to Me. It's about using your words to build others up, not tear them down.

It means standing up for what's right, even when you're standing alone. It means speaking truth, even when it's not the easiest path. It's about being a girl of your word, a girl who can be trusted. It means being honest, even when it's hard. It means keeping your promises, even when it's inconvenient.

Each choice you make is like a writing a sentence in your life's story. Choose words and actions that will make you proud when you see the whole story unfold.

I know there will be times when you mess up. But remember, when you stumble, I'm right there to pick you up, dust you off, and help you keep going.

So keep learning, keep growing, and keep leaning into My love. As you do, you'll find yourself becoming more and more the authentic, truth-filled girl I've created you to be.

I'm so proud of you, precious daughter. I see your heart. The world needs girls like you - girls who are brave enough to live with authenticity, with gentleness, truth, and integrity. Girls who change the world, not by being perfect, but by being perfectly Mine.

28
YOU ARE WISE

My beautiful daughter,

Did you know that I have already given you wisdom? Not the kind of wisdom that comes from books or grades or being "smart," but something far more precious - My wisdom that comes from knowing Me. I give wisdom to those who please me.

When you understand how strong and powerful I am, when you grasp even a glimpse of My awesome power and endless love, that's the beginning of true wisdom.

Imagine standing at the edge of the ocean or looking up at the stars. And then you remember that I am the One who flung those stars into space. Now can you begin to understand how vast and amazing I am, and yet I still choose to make My home in your heart?

This kind of wisdom I give you is a gift, and it's so much more than just knowing what's right. It's about having insight for every situation, knowing what to do when life gets confusing. When your friends are pulling you one way, when decisions feel overwhelming, when you're not sure which path to take -

remember, My wisdom is already within you, ready to guide you.

The world might tell you that wisdom comes from experience, from making mistakes, from figuring things out on your own. But true wisdom? It comes from staying close to Me. Like a flower turning toward the sun, when you keep your heart turned toward Me, I will give you wisdom and understanding beyond your years.

My wisdom brings so many blessings: peace when others are anxious, clarity when others are confused, understanding when others can't see the way forward. As you learn to recognise My voice in your heart, you'll find yourself making choices that might not make sense to others but lead to life and joy.

You don't have to try to be wise by your own strength. You don't have to have all the answers. You don't have to figure everything out - you just need to stay close to Me.

Remember, precious one: I have placed My wisdom within you. Let that truth sink deep into your heart today.

I love to give wisdom generously to those of my children who ask for it. It's My delight to guide you. So, when you need wisdom, Simply pause, take a breath, and ask Me for it.

29
YOU ARE FREE

My beloved child,

I have set you free - free to be exactly who I created you to be. I paid the ultimate price to set you free from the chains of sin and expectation, so that you could walk in freedom. (Galatians 5:1)

In a world that constantly bombards you with messages about who you should be, what you should look like, and what you should achieve, I invite you to find your identity and worth in Me alone.

When comparison tempts you to doubt your worth, remember: that's not your destiny. I have made you unique, with your own special blend of gifts and passions. Embrace the masterpiece that is you. (Ephesians 2:10)

When you catch yourself measuring your worth against others, remember that comparison can steal your joy. Don't try to fit into a mould that was never meant for you. That's not your destiny.

I have made you unique, with your own special blend of gifts and passions. Embrace the masterpiece that is you. (Ephesians 2:10)

The world may try to squeeze you into its image. But you don't have to strive for anyone's acceptance or validation. You already have My unconditional love and approval.

Instead, fix your attention on Me and you'll be changed from the inside out. (Romans 12:2 MSG) As you spend time with Me, I will shape your heart and mind to reflect Mine. Living in alignment with My will is what brings true freedom.

When others try to pressure you to conform, remember that you belong to Me. There will be many voices vying for your attention, telling you what you should be. But I invite you to tune your heart to My voice above all others. You are not a slave to the expectations of others. You are free.

Freedom doesn't mean doing whatever you want; it means having the liberty to become all I created you to be. It's the freedom to love with My love, to serve with My strength, to live with My purpose. True freedom is found in surrender to Me, for it is in losing your life that you truly find it. (Matthew 16:25)

I delight in you, not because of what you do, but because of who you are. You are a daughter of the King, royalty in My eyes. You are My beloved child.

So, hold your head high, in the quiet confidence of knowing who you are. I know you completely and will love you forever. So, walk in the freedom of being led by My Spirit. (Galatians 5:18)

My precious girl, embrace the freedom that is yours in Me. Dance to the beat of the unique drum I've placed within you.

Laugh freely, love deeply, and live life to the fullest, knowing that you are fearfully and wonderfully made, designed to experience the joy and freedom.

Now go and live! Embrace the freedom I've given you to live a life of purpose, a life that reflects the incredible girl I created you to be.

30
YOU ARE CHERISHED

My cherished daughter,

I have loved you with an everlasting love. (Jeremiah 31:3) This love surrounds you always, no matter what your situation looks like.

Every life journey is different, and I see the unique challenges you face in yours. Some days might be filled with joy and laughter, while others might bring tears and frustration. I'm with you through it all - the good times and the difficult ones. (Deuteronomy 31:6)

When people hurt you or let you down, it's okay to feel sad or angry. Bring those feelings to me. I'm always here to listen and comfort you. Remember, even if others disappoint you, I never will. I am your constant source of love and support. (Psalm 27:10)

It's not always easy and it's okay to set boundaries and seek help when you need it.

If you have people in your life who are loving and supportive, cherish them. They are precious gifts. Encourage them, build them up, and let them know you appreciate them. (1 Thessalonians 5:11)

I want you to know that love and support can come from unexpected places. Sometimes, the people I place in your life include those who aren't related to you. These might be close friends, a teacher who looks out for you, or a neighbour who cares. They're the ones who support you, encourage you, and show you love. (Proverbs 17:17)

I've placed these special people in your life for a reason. They're part of my plan for you, an extension of my love. They can be a source of joy, strength, and comfort, especially when life is difficult.

Remember how I adopted you into my family? In the same way, you can embrace those I've placed around you as part of your support system. Love isn't limited - it grows wherever it's nurtured. (Ephesians 1:5)

When life feels overwhelming, lean on me. I am your rock, your refuge, your ever-present help in trouble. (Psalm 46:1) Bring all your joys and struggles to me in prayer. I'm always here, ready to listen and help.

You play a special role in the lives of those around you. Your kindness, your forgiveness, your joy can make a difference, even in small ways. Let my love flow through you, but also remember to be gentle with yourself.

No matter what your life looks like - always remember that you are part of my family. You are my cherished child, loved beyond measure. Nothing can ever change that. (Romans 8:38-39)

31
YOU ARE ENOUGH

My treasured one,

Through My Son Jesus, I have already given you everything. Every spiritual blessing, every promise, every good gift - they're all yours. You don't have to work for them or earn them. They're yours because you're Mine.

Do you know what this means? It means you're free! Free from having to prove yourself. Free from striving to be good enough. Free from trying to earn My love. My Son has already paid the full price to give you this freedom. (Galatians 5:1)

I love watching you grow and bloom into all I've created you to be. But this growth isn't about struggling to become worthy - you already are loved and accepted by me. It's about living in the fullness of everything I've already given you. Like a garden bursting into bloom, you're simply becoming who you already are in Me.

When you accepted My gift of salvation, all My promises became yours. All My power became available to you. All My love was poured out into your heart through My Spirit. You don't need to earn these gifts – they're already yours.

There may be days when you feel weak, when you stumble, when you fall or fail. But even then, My grace is sufficient for you, for My power is made perfect in weakness. (2 Corinthians 12:9) Your weakness doesn't diminish your worth – it simply creates space for My strength to shine through you.

There is no pressure to be perfect from Me. I'm not standing at a distance watching for your mistakes or measuring your performance. I'm right here beside you, My arms wrapped around you, delighting in who you are and celebrating every step of who you're becoming.

This life isn't about striving - it's a joyful adventure of discovering all the treasures I've already placed within you. Each day brings new chances to unwrap more of the beautiful gifts of who I've created you to be.

So, rest in My love today. Breathe deeply of My grace. Let go of the striving, the performing, the endless trying to measure up. In Me, you are enough. You always have been. You always will be.

My beloved child, as you close this book, carry this truth with you always: You are enough because I am enough. You are complete in Me. And though I will keep working in your life – creating beauty, bringing healing, revealing strength – it's all built on rock-solid truth: You, my precious daughter, are already fully loved, completely accepted, and eternally cherished.

Now lift your head high. Walk forward in confidence. Live in my freedom. For you are Mine, you are loved, and you are enough.

YOUR STORY CONTINUES

The story God is writing in your life is just beginning. Each day is a new chapter where His love surrounds, His grace unfolds, and His plans for you come to life.

You are deeply loved, uniquely created, and infinitely precious. You are cherished, chosen, and empowered to shine brightly in this world, exactly as you are.

Remember, you are His masterpiece. So embrace your worth, walk in His grace, and let His love guide you.

Your story continues, and it is beautiful.

So, step boldly into your story, knowing that the Author of all things is walking beside you, cheering you on every step of the way.

AN INVITATION

Maybe as you've been reading these letters from your heavenly Father, you've felt His love tugging at your heart? Perhaps you're wondering how to accept His invitation to become part of His family?

God loves you so much that He sent His Son Jesus to bring you into His family. The Bible tells us: *"God loved the world so much that he gave his only Son, so that everyone who believes in him will have eternal life and never be lost."* (John 3:16 MSG)

If you'd like to begin your own relationship with God and become His child forever, you can talk to Him right now.

Here's a simple prayer to help you:

Lord Jesus,

Thank you for loving me just as I am

I am sorry for living life my own way

Thank you that you died for me, rose from the dead, and are alive today

Please forgive me and make me new

I invite you into my life—fill me with your Holy Spirit

I choose to follow you today and always

Amen

If you just prayed this prayer, welcome to God's family! You are now His precious child, and He will always love you. Everything you've read in this book about God's love for you is yours forever.

God's Holy Spirit now lives in you, giving you the strength and power to live this new life. Remember, your heavenly Father will be with you every step of the way as you begin this wonderful new journey with Him.

What's Next?

Here are some simple ways to grow closer to God:

- *Tell a Christian friend* or family member about your decision to follow Jesus
- *Start reading* your Bible - you can get a physical Bible or download a Bible app
- *Find a church* where you can make friends and learn more about God
- *Talk to God* every day - just like you'd talk to a friend

God has wonderful plans for your life as you get to know Him better!

ONE MORE THING

I appreciate the time you've taken to read this book. As an author, it means a lot to me!

If you have 60 seconds, hearing your honest feedback on Amazon would mean the world to me. It does wonders for the book, and I love to hear about your experience with it.